Adèle Geras
Ritchie's Rabbit

Illustrated by Vanessa Julian-Ottie

Hamish Hamilton·London

For Andrew and Hannah Szeftel

First published 1986
Published by Hamish Hamilton Children's Books
Garden House 57–59 Long Acre London WC2E 9JZ
Text copyright © 1986 by Adèle Geras
Illustrations copyright © 1986 by Vanessa Julian-Ottie
All Rights Reserved

British Library Cataloguing in Publication Data
Geras, Adèle
Ritchie's rabbit.
I. Title
823'.914[J]   PZ7
ISBN 0–241–11801–8

Printed in Great Britain by
Cambus Litho, East Kilbride
Typeset by Katerprint Co., Ltd, Cowley

Ritchie was rolling out some dough. The other children in the playgroup were painting, building towers and tall ships from coloured bricks, and whooshing down the slide.

Ritchie took the rabbit-shaped pastry-cutter and pressed it down on to the stretchy, springy, pale yellow dough, and there was a rabbit.

The rabbit sat sideways on the pastry-board with one ear pointing straight up and one ear bent over a little.

Ritchie gave the rabbit a red bead for an eye. "You're a nice rabbit," he said. "I'll take you home to show my Mum and Dad."

Then Ritchie went off to climb to the top of the climbing frame. The rabbit saw him waving from high, high up.

The rabbit looked at the children with his red glass eye. With his bent-over ear, he heard the song a little girl was singing to her doll as she put her to bed.

And with his straight ear he could hear two children shouting at one another over the top of the rolling-barrel.

On Thursdays, Ritchie's Dad always came to take him home. Just as they were going through the door, Ritchie remembered his rabbit, and ran back to get him. Would he still be there? Had he been cleared away? No, there he was.

Ritchie pushed the rabbit into his pocket and ran to catch up with his Dad. They went into the sweet shop together and Ritchie chose a bar of chocolate for his Thursday treat, to eat after lunch.

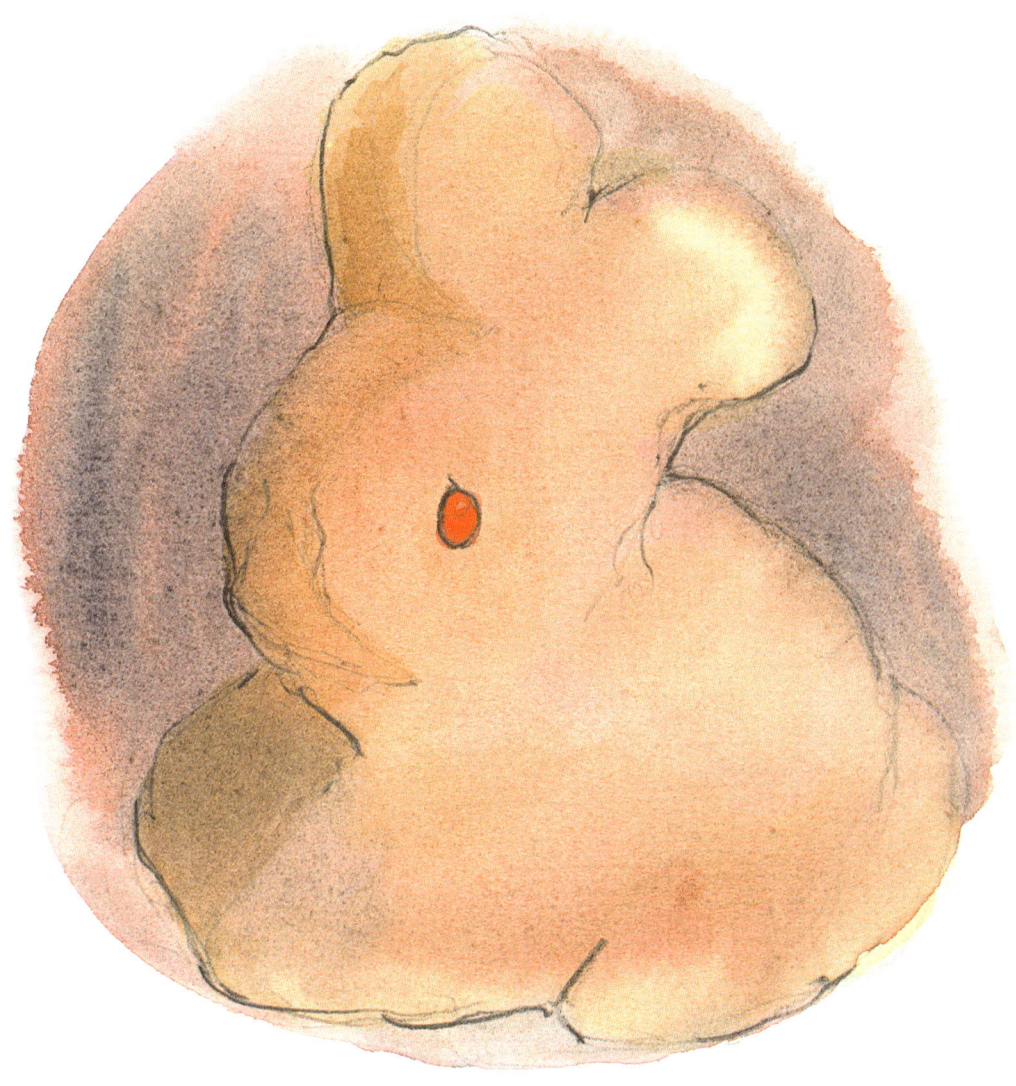

The rabbit did not like this new, dark place. His ears had been squeezed out of shape, and his body had become lumpy and bumpy.

There were strange things all around him: a small glass ball filled with swirly spirals of colour, a tangle of string, a muddy stone and a green leaf. With his bent-over ear, he could hear voices, and with his straight ear he heard the roar of an engine. The rabbit longed for the light.

When they reached home, Ritchie swung a few times on the garden gate. "You play here for a bit," said Dad, "while I go and get things ready."

Soon, Ritchie and his Dad were sitting at the kitchen table, having lunch.

They had ham and salad, and baked potatoes with lots of butter, and peaches from a tin. "My rabbit would like some lettuce," said Ritchie.
"Which rabbit?" said Dad.
"The rabbit in my pocket," said Ritchie. "The one I made at playgroup."

He took the rabbit out of his pocket and put him on the table. The dough was so squashed and dirty that Ritchie very nearly cried.

"He's all spoiled and horrid," said Ritchie. "He doesn't look like a rabbit any more. He looks like a grey lump of dough. He was such a lovely rabbit. I wanted to show him to you and Mum."
Dad took the dishes to the sink.

"Don't worry, Ritchie," he said, "when I've done the dishes, we'll find a way to make him into a rabbit again."

Ritchie sat at the table making patterns in the sugar bowl with his spoon. His Dad could do a lot of things, but Ritchie knew that there was no rabbit-shaped pastry-cutter in the kitchen drawer.

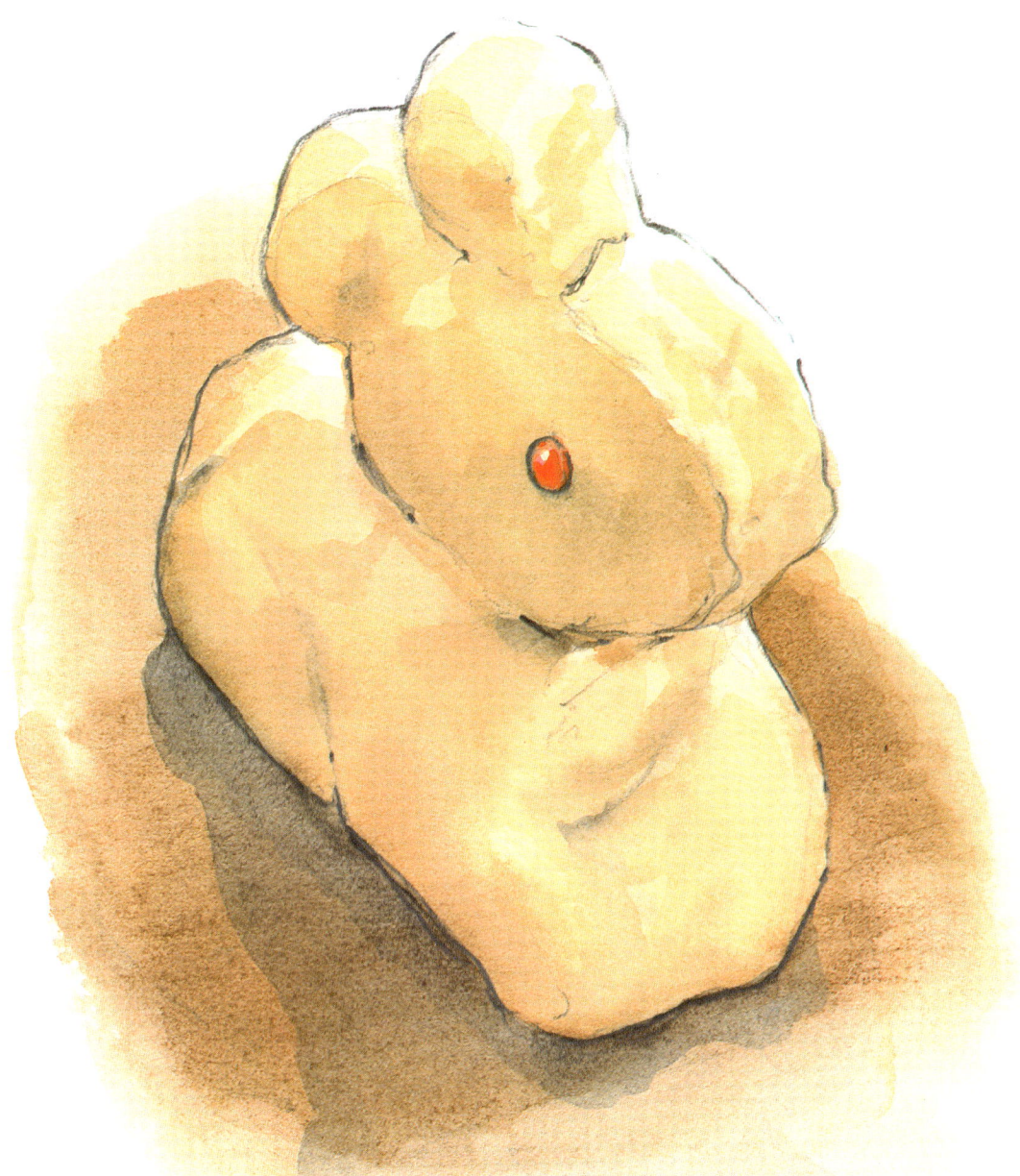

When he heard that he was to be made into a proper rabbit again, the squashed-up rabbit-lump cheered up a lot. He liked the clean shiny table he was on,

and he liked the bright plates and striped mugs standing in the dish-drainer.

A piece of lettuce had fallen near him, and he could smell the greenness and the wetness of it even though his nose had been pushed out of shape.

With his bent ear, he could hear the splash of water, and with his straight ear, the silvery tinkle of knives and forks. This was much better.

When the lunch things had been cleared away, Ritchie watched through the window as his Dad went into the back garden to fetch an apron from the washing line.

"We're ready to start now," Dad said when he came in

First, he shook out some flour. Then he rolled the grey dough around in the flour until it was a ball again, just as it had been at the beginning.

After that, he began to roll the ball flat with a rolling-pin.

"That's what I did too, Dad,"
said Ritchie, "but we haven't got a
rabbit-shaped pastry-cutter."
Dad scratched his nose
with a floury finger.
"Oh dear," he said.

"I know," said Ritchie suddenly. "I'll get the rabbit out of the jigsaw: the wooden one, then we can cut round that."
"I was just going to suggest that myself," said Dad.
Ritchie fetched the jigsaw rabbit and put it down on the dough.

Dad began to cut round it carefully.
"It's smaller than my rabbit," said Ritchie.
"Then we'll make two rabbits," said Dad.
"They'll be company for each other."

When both rabbits were cut out, Ritchie drew smiling mouths for them,

and Dad stuck currants into the dough for eyes.

He put the rabbits on a baking tray and turned on the oven. "We'll cook them," he told Ritchie, "and then they won't be squashy any more."

A few minutes later, two golden rabbits came out of the oven, winking black eyes.
"Smashing!" said Ritchie. "Thanks ever so much."
"Let's put them on a plate," said Dad, "and put the plate on your chest of drawers. They won't get broken there."

"I'm glad they're two rabbits," said Ritchie.
"Yes, they can talk together," said Dad.
"This plate looks like a field full of flowers," said Ritchie.

"They'll play together in this field I think, and they'll live happily on the flowered plate for ever and ever. They'll never quarrel."
"Why won't they quarrel then?" said Dad.
"Because," said Ritchie, "they'll remember that before we cooked them, they used to be just one rabbit."